BENCHED
DEALING WITH SPORTS INJURIES

WHAT IF I GET A SPRAIN?

 Gareth Stevens
PUBLISHING

 BY ERIKA EDWARDS

Please visit our website, www.garethstevens.com. For a free color catalog of all our high-quality books, call toll free 1-800-542-2595 or fax 1-877-542-2596.

Library of Congress Cataloging-in-Publication Data

Names: Edwards, Erika, author.
Title: What if I get a sprain? / Erika Edwards.
Description: New York : Gareth Stevens Publishing, [2016] | Series: Benched:
   dealing with sports injuries | Includes bibliographical references and
   index.
Identifiers: LCCN 2016015552 | ISBN 9781482448955 (pbk. book) | ISBN
   9781482448894 (library bound book) | ISBN 9781482448436 (6 pack)
Subjects: LCSH: Sprains–Juvenile literature. | Sports injuries–Juvenile
   literature. | Joints–Wounds and injuries–Juvenile literature.
Classification: LCC RD106 .E39 2016 | DDC 617.1/7–dc23
LC record available at https://lccn.loc.gov/2016015552

First Edition

Published in 2017 by
Gareth Stevens Publishing
111 East 14th Street, Suite 349
New York, NY 10003

Designer: Katelyn E. Reynolds
Editor: Ryan Nagelhout

Photo credits: Cover, p. 1 (background photo) Rena Schild/Shutterstock.com; cover, p. 1 (boy)
Digital Media Pro/Shutterstock.com; cover, pp. 1–24 (background texture) mexrix/Shutterstock.com;
cover, pp. 1–24 (chalk elements) Aleks Melnik/Shutterstock.com; p. 5 Gabe Souza/Portland Press Herald
via Getty Images; p. 7 Syda Productions/Shutterstock.com; p. 9 bikeriderlondon/Shutterstock.com;
p. 13 Syldavia/E+/Getty Images; p. 15 JPC-PROD/Shutterstock.com; p. 17 Adam Burn/Getty Images;
p. 19 Hero Images/Getty Images; p. 21 Doug Pensinger/Getty Images.

Printed in the United States of America

CPSIA compliance information: Batch #CS16GS : For further information contact Gareth Stevens, New York, New York at 1-800-542-2595.

CONTENTS

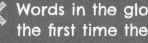
Words in the glossary appear in **bold** type
the first time they are used in the text.

WHAT A PAIN!

Your slap shot probably isn't as hard as that of hockey superstar Sidney Crosby. And it's unlikely you can hit home runs like David Ortiz. There are many ways **professional** athletes are different from us, but there's one way we're all the same: we all get sports **injuries** that hurt!

Both Crosby and Ortiz have had sprains that caused them to miss games. A sprain is a common sports injury, but what exactly is it? And how does it affect your ability to get back in the game?

THE GAME PLAN

1. Different injuries can affect different body parts. A sprain, for example, can happen almost anywhere on the body. Arms, ankles, and even backs can get sprained.

It's important to pay attention out on the field and on the ice, but sometimes falls and spills happen no matter how safely you play!

BANDS THAT HOLD

Sprains happen when ligaments **stretch** or tear. Ligaments attach bones to each other and keep joints together. They're made up of **connective tissue**. They're **flexible** and tough and help the body when it needs to move. But when a ligament is overworked, it can cause a sprain.

Think of your ligaments as rubber bands. When the bands are strong, they hold things together easily. Overused rubber bands, however, might tear or lose flexibility and toughness. But ligaments are different from rubber bands: With **treatment**, they can get better!

✗ THE GAME PLAN

You might think ligaments are part of the muscular system, but they're actually part of your skeletal system. They help the bones that make up your skeleton stay in place.

Just like exercise bands, your ligaments are strong and long-lasting tools your body needs to work safely.

7

HOW DO YOU KNOW?

Imagine you're running fast toward home plate. You slide in to beat the catcher's tag, but your leg gets caught under your body. Then something twists, and maybe you hear a popping noise. You'd better tell an adult, because you might have sprained your leg.

Hearing a popping noise is one of the warning signs of a sprain. You could also have pain, swelling in the area, or bruising. The sprain might make it hard to move, too.

✖ THE GAME PLAN

1 There are 900 ligaments in the human body.
That's a lot of different places to get a sprain.

A good way to make sure you don't hurt yourself when sliding is to learn the right way to do it. Ask your coach for tips so you learn how to play safely.

SPRAINS VS. STRAINS

What's the difference between a sprain and a strain? They have some things in common, but the biggest difference is that sprains affect joints and ligaments, while strains affect muscles.

Sprains often happen because of extreme stress placed on a joint at one time. Strains can happen over time. For example, if a gymnast has bad form while landing flips and jumps and lands on the wrong part of the foot enough times, a strain can develop.

WHAT'S THE DIFFERENCE?

SPRAINS

affects ligaments/joints, three grades (types) of injury

painful, bruising, treated with rest, ice, compression, and elevation

STRAINS

affects muscles, two kinds of injury: chronic (over time) and acute (starting suddenly)

DEGREES OF INJURY

Now that we know the part twisting and stretching ligaments plays in the sprain game, it's time to talk about the different levels of sprains. A sprain is ranked by its level of **severity**. There are three levels, called grades.

A grade 1 sprain might just be a mild twist of an ankle, but a grade 3 sprain is a serious injury that may mean a torn ligament. Any sprain needs to be reported to an adult, who can help you see a doctor.

✖ THE GAME PLAN

1 More than two-thirds of ligaments are in the arms and legs. The rest are in your neck and the middle of your body.

A doctor is usually needed to decide a sprain's severity, but all sprains hurt!

SPRAIN SEVERITY

Here are the three different levels of sprain.

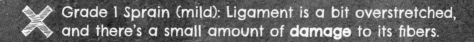 Grade 1 Sprain (mild): Ligament is a bit overstretched, and there's a small amount of **damage** to its fibers.

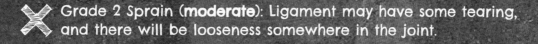 Grade 2 Sprain (**moderate**): Ligament may have some tearing, and there will be looseness somewhere in the joint.

Grade 3 Sprain (severe): Ligament is torn, and you won't be able to use the joint that's been sprained.

13

A TRIP TO THE DOCTOR

A sprain puts people on the bench right away. After a coach or trainer checks you out, you might need to visit your doctor. Your doctor will look at the color of your skin, the amount of swelling in the injured area, and how much you can move the sprained area.

If your ankle is injured, they might check to see if you can still walk. When you have a sprain, there's always a chance you have other injuries. Let the doctor know if you have any pain anywhere else.

✗ THE GAME PLAN

1. Your doctor may take X rays of your injured joint. These special pictures help check for injuries such as broken bones or other problems.

Your doctor will be the best person to get you on the fast track to healing after an injury.

15

FEELING NICE WITH R.I.C.E.!

After ruling out other injuries, your doctor will probably tell you to use R.I.C.E. No, not the white flaky food. R.I.C.E. is an **acronym** that stands for rest, ice, compression, and elevation. Let's break it down, so you understand each step in case you need them!

1. Rest: It means just what it sounds like! Your body needs time to heal, and resting your injury will always help this.

2. Ice: Ice keeps the swelling and bruising down after a sprain. You should ice a sprain as soon as possible.

3. Compression: Wrapping the injured area will help keep swelling down and keep your injured joint from moving too much.

4. Elevate: Try to keep your injury elevated, or raised, above your heart. This can also limit swelling.

✗ THE GAME PLAN

A doctor, Gabe Mirkin, came up with the R.I.C.E system in 1978!

R.I.C.E. your sprain, and you'll be back in the game in no time!

ONE SPRAIN IS ENOUGH

Even after you've recovered from a sprain, there's a good chance it can happen again. Reinjury is common with sprains, but you can take steps to avoid hitting the bench again.

Warming up before you play and being careful not to make unexpected movements with your injured body part can help prevent injury. Make sure you wear proper safety gear, too. For example, maybe you want to lace your hockey skates a little tighter after an ankle injury to better support the area.

✗ THE GAME PLAN

Sports equipment is always getting better to protect you. For example, some of today's basketball shoes rest higher on the ankle to offer more support during a game.

HOW TO PREVENT SPRAINS

 use proper safety gear

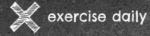 exercise daily

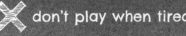 don't play when tired or in pain

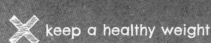 stretch

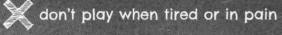 keep a healthy weight

Make sure you take care of yourself as much as you can by learning the correct way to stretch and doing it every time you play sports!

SHAUN'S SOCHI SCARE

Whether you're on the playground or at the Olympics, sprains can happen to athletes of every skill level. In 2013, professional snowboarder Shaun White was forced to sit out an Olympic **qualifying** event when he suffered a sprained ankle.

Shaun had just taken his first run on the half-pipe when he fell and twisted his ankle. His sprain made it much harder for him to make the 2014 games, which were held in Sochi, Russia, the next year.

✖ THE GAME PLAN

Shaun did end up competing in the 2014 Winter Olympics, but not at his usual level. He finished fourth in the half-pipe event, which he won at the previous two Olympic Games!

Shaun's Olympic hopes came crashing into the snow as he twisted an ankle!

GLOSSARY

acronym: a word made from the first letter of each word in a group of other words

connective tissue: matter inside the body that helps hold the body together and support the parts inside the body

damage: loss or harm caused by something

flexible: able to bend or move easily

injury: hurt or harm

moderate: neither very good or bad

professional: having to do with getting paid to do something

qualify: to make a special group or team

severity: the level of seriousness of something

stretch: to extend past normal use

treatment: a way or form of treating someone in order to heal them

FOR MORE INFORMATION

BOOKS
Landau, Elaine. *Sprains and Strains.* New York, NY: Marshall Cavendish Benchmark, 2011.

Ollhoff, Jim. *Muscles and Bones.* Edina, MN: ABDO Publishing, 2012.

WEBSITES

Sprains and Strains
www.nlm.nih.gov/medlineplus/sprainsandstrains.html
Learn more about why sprains and strains happen here.

Strains and Sprains Are a Pain
kidshealth.org/en/kids/strains-sprains.html
Find more information about strains and sprains for kids here.

INDEX